The Heart of Hustle

A Story of Business, Love, and Everything In Between

SHUBHAM SHAURAV

In business, as in love, the real magic happens when we dare to take risks and trust the proces

Contents

Foreword

In the fast-paced world of entrepreneurship, where every decision feels like a make-or-break moment, it's easy to forget the heart behind the hustle. Entrepreneurs often juggle endless deadlines, client demands, and the pressure of scaling businesses. But behind every successful venture is a journey of personal growth, relationships, and the constant battle between ambition and vulnerability.

The Heart of Hustle tells the story of Ravi, an entrepreneur navigating not just the complexities of his SaaS business, but also the intricacies of human connection. Ravi's story resonates with anyone who's had to make difficult choices between professional ambition and personal emotions. As his path crosses with Pooja, a long-lost friend and seasoned marketing consultant, their professional partnership begins to blossom into something more meaningful. Together, they face the ups and downs of building a business and a relationship, learning that the two are not as separate as they might seem.

Through moments of vulnerability, strategic growth, and quiet introspection, The Heart of Hustle illustrates that no matter how driven we are, our relationships whether professional or romantic are central to our success. It's a reminder that, while the road to building a business may be paved with hard work and determination, it's often the people we meet along the way who make the journey worthwhile.

In reading this story, you'll not only explore the fundamentals of lead generation, content marketing, and cold outreach, but you'll also see how these business strategies parallel the personal lessons of trust, patience, and growth. Whether you're an entrepreneur or someone seeking a balance between life's ambitions and relationships, this book will resonate on multiple levels.

As you turn these pages, may you be reminded that the heart behind every hustle is what truly drives success.

Preface

Every journey, whether in life, love, or business, has its turning points. Moments that challenge our comfort zone, make us question our beliefs, and push us toward growth. This story is about one such journey where business ambition collides with personal connection, and both lead to unexpected transformation.

At its core, this book follows the journey of Ravi, a B2B entrepreneur who finds himself at a crossroads. His startup is struggling, and he's feeling the weight of investor pressure and his own uncertainty. Just when things seem to be unraveling, a familiar face re-enters his life: Pooja, a long-lost friend and now a sharp marketing consultant. What begins as a professional collaboration soon becomes something more, as Ravi not only learns to navigate his business challenges but also rediscovers emotions he had long buried.

This book weaves together themes of entrepreneurship, personal growth, and romance, illustrating how deeply interconnected they can be. While Ravi learns the business strategies necessary to take his SaaS product to the next level, he also finds himself learning about trust, vulnerability, and the delicate balance between the heart and mind.

As you read, you'll see that this is not just a story of building a successful business. It's a story of personal evolution of learning that success in life doesn't come from simply hitting business milestones, but from the relationships we nurture and the connections that help us grow. Ravi's journey is both a professional and emotional one, and through it, we explore how love and business can sometimes follow surprisingly similar paths.

This book was written for anyone who has ever found themselves balancing multiple aspects of their lives and wondering how it all fits together. It is for entrepreneurs, dreamers, and those who believe that life's greatest successes are born from the courage to follow both your passion and your heart.

Shubham Shaurav

1. The Breaking Point

Ravi sat at his desk, staring blankly at the blinking cursor on his laptop screen. It was a cruel reminder of everything that wasn't happening no notifications, no sales, no leads. His once-promising SaaS business, a tool designed to streamline project management for teams, was floundering. He had launched it with the optimism of a young entrepreneur, believing it would fill a gap in the market, revolutionise workflows, and ultimately make his mark in the industry. But instead of success, he found himself in an endless cycle of frustration, watching his ambitious dream unravel.

At 30, Ravi was supposed to be hitting his stride. He had spent the last five years building his business from the ground up, sacrificing sleep, personal time, and relationships, all for the vision of creating something impactful. But as he sat there now, his once unshakable belief in his product felt foolish. He had followed the playbook invested in paid ads, poured resources into email campaigns, hired agencies to run webinars, and even tried cold outreach. But nothing seemed to work.

The notifications from his investor group were piling up in his inbox, each one more pointed than the last. *"Where are the results, Ravi? What's your plan for this quarter? We need to see growth."* The pressure was suffocating.

His runway was shrinking, and the fear of failure loomed larger with each passing day.

He rubbed his temples, feeling the onset of a headache. The same nagging thought kept returning: *What am I missing?* He had always prided himself on being proactive, the kind of entrepreneur who left no stone unturned. But no matter how many marketing strategies he tried, the leads trickled in like a slow drip from a faulty faucet. Conversion rates were embarrassingly low, and the burn rate on his marketing budget was a constant source of anxiety.

Sitting in the dimly lit room, Ravi couldn't help but reflect on how far he had drifted from the excitement he'd once felt about his startup. In the early days, everything had felt possible. The product had garnered good feedback during its beta phase, and the initial traction had made him believe that success was just around the corner. But as time went on, the honeymoon phase ended. The uphill battle of acquiring customers and converting them into loyal users had become an all-consuming challenge.

Exhausted and overwhelmed, Ravi's thoughts spiraled into doubt. *Was this the end of the road? Had he miscalculated? Was his idea just not good enough?*

The sound of his phone buzzing pulled him out of his reverie. Half-expecting another email from his investors or some automated marketing alert, he reached for the device without much enthusiasm. His eyes widened when he saw the name on the screen: *Pooja.*

His heart skipped a beat. He hadn't heard from her in years. Pooja, his old friend from university. The last time they had spoken, it had been during the rush of final exams, a lifetime ago or so it felt. They had been close, closer than he had ever been with anyone. There had always been something special between them, a connection that felt effortless, as if they were meant to understand each other. Their long conversations, the late-night study sessions, the laughter they had chemistry. Not just the intellectual kind, but something unspoken that neither of them had ever really addressed.

Back then, Ravi had always found an excuse not to act on his feelings. There had been too much going on college, career plans, and the looming uncertainty of the future. And then, after graduation, life had taken them in different directions. Pooja had gone abroad for her MBA, and Ravi had dived headfirst into the entrepreneurial world in Mumbai. Distance, time, and the pursuit of their individual dreams had slowly eroded their connection until it faded completely.

Now, out of nowhere, there she was.

Ravi opened the message, feeling a strange mix of anticipation and nostalgia.

"Hey Ravi, long time! I came across your company the other day and remembered all the times we used to talk about our big plans back in college. How's everything going? I'm working as a B2B marketing consultant now and thought maybe we could catch up. Let me know if you

need help with lead generation seriously, I'd love to chat. :)"

He read the message twice, then a third time, his mind racing. *Pooja, a B2B consultant?* Of course, she had always been ambitious and driven, but somehow the idea of her in this new role caught him off guard. He couldn't help but wonder if the message was purely business, or if there was something more behind it. Was she genuinely interested in reconnecting, or was this just another consulting pitch?

Ravi leaned back in his chair, letting the memories wash over him. He thought back to those endless nights in the university library when they had studied side by side, challenging each other with questions, daring each other to dream bigger. It had always been Pooja's laughter that broke through the tension, her ability to make even the most stressful situations feel lighter.

They had been so close then, but life happened. The distance grew as Pooja went off to Europe for her studies. Their conversations had tapered off, replaced by quick texts and sporadic updates on social media. Eventually, even those had stopped. He had always wondered what might have happened if things had been different. If he had taken the chance to pursue something more with her. But now, she was practically a stranger.

A stranger offering help.

The irony wasn't lost on him. Here he was, at one of the lowest points in his entrepreneurial journey, and out of nowhere, the person who had once been his closest confidant had reappeared, offering a lifeline. He couldn't help but feel skeptical, though. After all, Pooja was a consultant now. She had her own agenda, her own goals. Maybe this was just business to her.

But as much as he tried to guard himself against that possibility, there was another part of him a part he hadn't acknowledged in years that wanted to believe this was more than just a business offer. That maybe, just maybe, fate was giving him another chance to reconnect with someone who had meant so much to him.

Ravi stared at his phone, his thumb hovering over the screen. What should he say? Should he take her up on the offer? He could use the help, no doubt about that. His lead generation efforts were in shambles, and if anyone could offer insight, it would be Pooja. She had always been sharp, always able to see things from angles he hadn't considered.

But at the same time, the thought of seeing her again, of opening that door, stirred something in him he wasn't sure he was ready to face.

Finally, after what felt like an eternity, he typed a reply.

"Hey Pooja! Wow, it really has been a long time. Crazy to think how much has changed since college. Things have been… challenging, to say the least. I could definitely use some help. How about we grab coffee this weekend and catch up?"

His thumb hovered over the send button for a moment. He wasn't sure if he was more nervous about the business conversation or seeing her again after all this time.

He hit send. There it was, out in the world. A small glimmer of hope in an otherwise dismal situation.

As he placed the phone back on the desk, Ravi couldn't shake the mix of emotions swirling inside him. He wasn't sure if this would turn out to be a business move, a personal reconnection, or something in between. But whatever it was, it felt like a shift, a potential turning point.

He leaned back in his chair, closing his eyes for a moment. Maybe this was the break he needed. Not just for his business, but for himself.

For the first time in weeks, Ravi allowed himself a small smile. It was faint, barely there, but it was something.

Little did he know, this message would mark the beginning of a journey that would challenge not only his business acumen but also his ability to navigate the complicated terrain of past relationships and missed opportunities. The road ahead was uncertain, but for the first time in a long time, Ravi felt like he wasn't completely alone in it.

2. Reconnecting with Pooja

The café was cozy and warm, a comforting space that contrasted sharply with the storm brewing in Ravi's mind. He had picked this place because it was near the university where so much of his life had changed. Now, he sat waiting for Pooja, his fingers nervously tapping the edge of his coffee cup. His mind wandered back to the memories of study sessions, where their bond had grown over shared laughter and stress-filled deadlines. Back then, Pooja was his friend, someone who understood him in ways no one else did. He had always wondered what might have happened if distance and life hadn't gotten in the way.

But today was different. She was meeting him not as an old friend, but as a consultant. The thought weighed heavily on him. Ravi wasn't sure how to balance the professional need for her advice with the personal connection he still longed to rebuild.

The bell above the door chimed, and Ravi's heart skipped a beat. There she was Pooja. She hadn't changed much physically. She still had the same radiant smile, though now it carried a cool, collected confidence. Her clothes were sharp, professional, and she walked with the ease of someone who had mastered her domain. The Pooja he knew had always been driven, but this Pooja—she was different. She had evolved into someone powerful, someone who seemed miles away from the late-night coffee and casual conversations they once shared.

"Ravi!" Pooja greeted him warmly, but there was something distant in her tone, like a switch had been flipped, keeping things formal.

"Pooja, you look…" Ravi fumbled for words as he stood to greet her. "You look amazing."

"Thanks," she said with a polite smile, taking the seat across from him. She seemed completely at ease, while Ravi felt like a bundle of nerves. He had hoped that meeting her again might rekindle some of the old feelings, but from the look in her eyes, this meeting was strictly business.

"So, tell me about what's going on," Pooja said, skipping the small talk entirely. She pulled out her phone, ready to take notes, her fingers poised over the screen.

Ravi's stomach dropped slightly. It wasn't the casual catch-up he had been hoping for. This was Pooja the consultant, and he felt like just another client in her day.

He took a deep breath, pushing aside his disappointment, and dived into the story of his SaaS business. "Things have been tough lately. My ad campaigns… they aren't working, and investors are starting to get impatient. I don't know where I'm going wrong."

Pooja listened, her face composed, nodding at all the right moments. She didn't interrupt, but her focus was laser-sharp. It was clear that she was listening as a consultant, assessing the situation with a detached professionalism. Ravi couldn't help but miss the way she used to listen as a friend, her expressions more open, her warmth more apparent.

"I've tried multiple ad platforms, hired agencies, changed messaging nothing's clicking. I feel like I'm shouting into the void, and no one's listening." Ravi's frustration came through in his voice, his fingers gripping the edge of the table.

Pooja paused, tilting her head slightly as she analyzed his words. "It sounds like you're running campaigns without a clear understanding of who your customer really is."

Ravi blinked. "I thought I had that down. I'm targeting startups, small teams that need better project management tools."

Pooja gave him a sympathetic smile, but it was the kind of smile a consultant gives before delivering hard truths. "That's too broad, Ravi. Think about it what kinds of startups? What stage are they in? Are they funded? Bootstrapped? What industry are they in? A general message to all startups won't resonate because their needs are different. You need to drill down into your Ideal Customer Profile."

As she spoke, she reached for a napkin and began to draw out a quick diagram, explaining how to segment the audience based on their pain points and decision-making stages. As their hands accidentally brushed while she took the napkin to draw out the concept, Ravi felt a sudden spark, the same old electricity from their past. He froze for a moment, his eyes flicking to hers to see if she felt it too. But Pooja didn't seem to react. If she noticed the contact, she was good at hiding it, her focus still entirely on the business at hand.

He wondered if he was reading too much into it. Was it just nostalgia on his part? After all, they were here for business weren't they?

"Your messaging needs to speak to specific problems," she continued, circling smaller segments of the napkin with her pen. "For instance, if you're targeting early-stage startups, their pain point is likely cash flow or scaling productivity quickly. A later-stage startup might care more about managing growth or optimizing workflows."

Ravi nodded, trying to focus on her words, but part of him couldn't shake the disappointment that had settled in his chest. He had hoped this meeting would bring back some of the connection they once had, but it was clear that Pooja was all business. She was here to help him, but not in the way he had hoped.

"So, I need to rethink my audience?" Ravi asked, trying to get back into the flow of the conversation.

"Exactly," Pooja said, leaning back in her chair. "You can't market effectively if you're targeting everyone. Start with a refined ICP know exactly who you're talking to, and tailor your campaigns to address their specific problems. It's about making them feel like you understand their pain and that your product is the solution."

Her words made sense, and Ravi appreciated the clarity she brought to the situation. But the personal connection he had longed for the one that had drawn him to Pooja in the first place felt out of reach. She was a professional through and through, and while she was helping him, it felt transactional.

As they continued talking, Ravi tried to steer the conversation toward more familiar ground. "Do you ever think about our old university days?" he asked, a slight smile on his face. "Those late-night study sessions, all the coffee we drank? Feels like a lifetime ago."

Pooja looked up from her phone, her expression softening for a brief moment. "Yeah, I remember. Those were good times. But things change, right?"

Ravi nodded, though her response wasn't what he had hoped for. "Yeah… things change."

As the conversation returned to business, Ravi couldn't help but feel the shift. The Pooja he had known was still in there somewhere, but she was guarded now, focused on her role as a consultant, not the friend he had once confided in.

They wrapped up the meeting with Pooja giving him actionable advice on refining his lead generation strategy. She offered to follow up with more detailed steps via email, her tone friendly but formal.

As she stood to leave, Ravi caught himself before he could ask her to stay a little longer, maybe grab dinner, or talk more about life. But the reality was clear Pooja was here on business. Nothing more.

"I'll send you those notes tonight," she said, flashing him one last professional smile. "You've got potential, Ravi. You just need to tighten your focus. We'll get you there."

"Thanks, Pooja," Ravi said, managing a smile in return. "I appreciate it."

And with that, she was gone, leaving Ravi sitting in the café with more clarity about his business but less certainty about the personal connection he had hoped to rekindle. Pooja was no longer the friend from study sessions. She was a consultant, and to her, he was just another client.

As he watched her disappear into the city, Ravi felt a familiar ache. Maybe he had hoped for too much. Maybe, in this world of business, some things were just better left in the past.

3. The Power of Knowing Your Audience

The café meeting had left Ravi in a daze. As he walked through the crowded city streets in the days that followed, his mind replayed their conversation over and over again. He couldn't shake the way Pooja's voice had shifted into that confident, no-nonsense tone, or how her eyes had lit up when she started talking strategy.

"Ravi, you're missing the point," she had said, her brows furrowing in concentration. "You're focusing on your product, but your audience doesn't even know they need it yet."

"I know," he had muttered, embarrassed by his blind spots. "But I thought if I just showed them what it does…"

"No." She had leaned forward, tapping the table with her finger for emphasis. "They need to feel their pain first. Only then will they care about your solution."

The way she could cut through the noise like that—it was something Ravi had always admired about her. He hadn't felt this motivated in months. But then, of course, there was that brief, fleeting touch when their hands had brushed, the spark that had left him thinking about something entirely different from business.

Ravi wasn't sure if Pooja had felt it, too. She hadn't reacted, continuing on with her ideas as if nothing had happened. For her, this was just another client meeting or at least that's what he kept telling himself. But for him? He felt an old pull he thought he'd left behind.

Unable to ignore the blend of excitement and curiosity, Ravi messaged Pooja the next day. He needed more than just advice he needed clarity, both on his business and what was happening between them.

"Hey Pooja," he typed, his fingers hovering over the keyboard for a second. "Thanks for all the help yesterday. Would love to dive deeper into my audience strategy. Coffee or dinner sometime soon?"

The message sounded casual enough, but he knew it carried more weight than he wanted to admit. To his relief, her response came in quickly:

"Dinner sounds good. How about we work at my place? Easier to focus there. Wednesday evening?"

Ravi agreed, trying to keep his excitement in check.

When Wednesday arrived, Ravi found himself standing outside Pooja's apartment, feeling a strange mix of anticipation and nervousness. The last time he had been this close to her world, they were still in college, dreaming big and wondering what the future held. And now? The stakes felt different. His business was at risk, and yet there was also something unspoken between them something that had never been addressed, even years ago.

The door opened, and Pooja welcomed him in with a warm smile. Her apartment was a perfect reflection of who she had become clean, organized, with sharp, minimalistic touches. A sleek desk with her laptop, a whiteboard, and scattered notes filled the living room. It was a far cry from the mess of textbooks and coffee cups that had once filled their study sessions.

"Come on in, make yourself at home," she said, moving toward the whiteboard. "I've got everything set up."

Ravi took a seat on her couch, still taking in the surroundings. Everything here felt calm, professional—so much like Pooja. She was different now, but he could still see glimpses of the girl he used to know in the way she moved with purpose.

As Pooja gathered her materials, she absentmindedly grabbed a pen, twirling it between her fingers. "So, Ravi," she began, her voice slipping into that familiar, authoritative tone that reminded him of why he had come. "Before we dive in, I want to ask you a few questions about your audience."

Ravi nodded, pulling out his notebook and trying to focus. "Yeah, I've been thinking about that since we last talked."

Pooja turned toward him, holding the pen in her mouth for a second as she gathered her thoughts. Then, she set it down and reached for a rubber band, pulling her hair back into a messy ponytail. "Good," she said, almost in teacher mode now. "But I don't think you've been asking yourself the right questions. Let's break it down."

She grabbed a marker and approached the whiteboard, pausing for a second. "First things first what stage of awareness is your audience in?"

Ravi hesitated. "Um, I guess they know they have a problem, but—"

"No guessing," Pooja interrupted, shaking her head and smiling as she tapped the board. "Let's be sure. There are different stages of awareness, remember? Some people don't even know they have a problem yet. Others know they have one but aren't sure what the solution is. Some are aware of solutions but don't know about your product, and a few might already be looking for exactly what you offer. You can't treat them all the same."

Ravi watched as she methodically sketched out the stages of awareness on the whiteboard, the marker moving with precision as she spoke. Her posture, the way she tied her hair back and stepped into a role that was equal parts consultant and mentor it was mesmerizing. It reminded him of the way she used to tutor him back in college, back when they had stayed up late, working through problems, laughing, and sharing thoughts about life.

But tonight was different. There was a tension in the air that Ravi couldn't quite place. She was deep into her explanation, completely in her element, but he found himself distracted not by what she was saying, but by her. The way she furrowed her brow when she got intense, the little pauses she took when trying to explain something complicated, even the way she absentmindedly chewed on her pen as she thought.

As she drew out the buyer's journey in neat circles, she reached for a napkin to jot down some extra notes. As their hands brushed again, the now-familiar spark ran through Ravi. He froze for a second, wondering if she felt it, too.

Pooja, seemingly unaffected, continued, her voice smooth and focused. "Here's where most businesses go wrong, Ravi," she said, her tone firm but gentle. "You're trying to speak to everyone at once, which means your message is landing with no one. Each of these stages requires different messaging. What you tell someone who's unaware of their problem is different from what you say to someone who's ready to buy."

Ravi nodded, trying to focus on her words, but his gaze lingered a moment too long on her. Pooja turned around just in time to catch him staring. For a split second, her expression softened, as if she had noticed the shift between them, but she quickly turned back to the whiteboard, brushing it off as nothing.

"Right," Ravi said, clearing his throat. "I see what you mean. I've been sending out the same message to everyone, hoping it sticks."

"Exactly," she said, tying her hair up even tighter and moving closer to him, holding out the pen. "But with what we're doing now, we'll fix that. We need to tailor each piece of your marketing to fit where your prospect is in their journey. Are they unaware? Talk about their pain. Are they solution-aware? Position your product as the answer they've been looking for. It's all about meeting them where they are."

Ravi took the pen from her, nodding. "That makes sense. I've been too broad."

Pooja smiled, her serious tone giving way to a softer, more personal one. "Don't worry. We'll get it right."

As the evening wore on, they worked through Ravi's target audience, mapping out strategies for each awareness stage. Pooja guided him through the process with ease, her business acumen on full display. But despite the professional atmosphere, the air between them felt thick with unspoken tension. Every time they exchanged glances, Ravi felt something stir something he had been trying to ignore.

At one point, Ravi found himself watching her again, admiring the way she could switch between serious and playful, between professional and personal. She caught him this time, too, but instead of brushing it off, her gaze lingered for just a second longer than it had before. There was something there, something neither of them were ready to address.

Finally, as the night drew to a close, Ravi packed up his things, still feeling the weight of that unspoken chemistry between them.

"You've got a solid foundation now," Pooja said, walking him to the door. "We'll pick up from here next time."

"Thanks, Pooja," Ravi replied, his voice a little softer than usual. "This has been really helpful."

Pooja smiled, but this time, there was a hint of something more behind her eyes a flicker of recognition that maybe, just maybe, the spark he was feeling wasn't one-sided after all.

As he left her apartment, Ravi couldn't help but wonder: Was this strictly business, or was there something more slowly building between them?

4. The Funnel and the Dinner

The next few days blurred together in a whirlwind of brainstorming sessions and strategic discussions. Pooja's apartment had become their impromptu office, with late-night whiteboard sessions, stacks of post-its, and cups of coffee that never seemed to run out. Every evening, Ravi found himself more engrossed in their work and in Pooja.

It wasn't just the business side of things that kept him coming back. There was something about being around her, the way she made everything seem less complicated. Her ability to break down complex marketing principles into simple, actionable steps was impressive. But more than that, there was an energy between them that Ravi couldn't ignore, a growing connection that hung in the air like static electricity, charging every glance and every touch.

One evening, after what felt like hours of dissecting buyer personas, Ravi leaned back on the couch, rubbing his eyes. "I think my brain's going to explode," he groaned, half-laughing.

Pooja chuckled, glancing at the clock. "We've been at this for a while. How about we take a break and grab dinner?

There's a small restaurant down the street that's pretty good."

Ravi hesitated for a moment, wondering if this was purely about food or if it meant something more. But he quickly pushed the thought away. "Dinner sounds great. I could use a change of scenery."

They packed up their materials, leaving the cluttered workspace behind, and headed out into the cool night air. As they walked to the restaurant, the conversation shifted away from business. The streets were quieter than usual, and for the first time in days, Ravi felt like he could breathe without thinking about audience funnels or messaging tactics.

Inside the restaurant, they found a cozy table near the window. It was a small place, dimly lit, with the scent of spices and garlic in the air. Pooja settled into her seat, glancing over the menu.

"So," she said, breaking the silence as she looked up at him, "how's everything else going? You've been so focused on work lately I imagine the pressure's getting to you."

Ravi sighed, leaning back in his chair. It was the first time in days anyone had asked him how he was doing beyond the business. "Yeah, I won't lie. The pressure's intense. The investors… they're not exactly patient. They want results, and fast. I feel like I'm constantly trying to catch up, like I'm sprinting just to stay in place."

Pooja nodded, her expression softening. "I get it. When I started out, it felt like I was constantly failing before I ever succeeded. No one tells you how much of this business stuff is about perseverance about getting back up after the hundredth setback."

Ravi was surprised at how easily she shared her story. "I didn't know that," he said. "You always seemed like you had it all figured out."

Pooja laughed lightly, shaking her head. "Far from it. I started from scratch after quitting a stable job. No savings, no backup plan just a lot of late nights and failed attempts. It wasn't glamorous, but it taught me a lot about resilience. I think that's why I'm so passionate about helping others now."

Her words hit home. Ravi found himself relaxing, the weight of his responsibilities easing as he listened to her talk about her journey. He hadn't expected this side of Pooja the vulnerability behind the confident exterior.

As they talked, Ravi noticed how comfortable he felt with her. He found himself laughing more easily, their conversation flowing seamlessly from work to life and back again. The way she spoke, the way she listened it felt effortless. There was a warmth between them now, something that had been simmering for days but was only now coming to the surface.

Midway through the meal, as they both reached for the menu to order dessert, their hands brushed again. This time, neither of them pulled away. There was no awkwardness, no fumbling apologies just a moment that hung between them, charged with something unspoken.

Ravi felt his pulse quicken, his eyes lingering on hers. Pooja didn't say anything, but there was a flicker of something in her gaze, something she quickly hid by glancing down at the menu again.

"So, about that funnel," she said, steering the conversation back to business. But her voice was softer now, and Ravi couldn't help but wonder if she was feeling the same pull he was.

Ravi cleared his throat, trying to focus. "Right, the funnel. I'm still trying to wrap my head around it."

Pooja leaned forward, her teacher mode switching back on. "Okay, think of it like this," she began, grabbing the napkin from the table and sketching out a quick diagram. "At the top, you have the Top of Funnel TOFU. This is where your prospects are just starting to become aware of their problem. They're not ready to buy yet, but they're curious. That's where you nurture them."

She circled the top part of the napkin. "You need to provide value here educate them, build trust. It's not about selling yet. You're warming them up, guiding them down the funnel."

Ravi nodded, finally beginning to understand. "And then, once they're warmed up?"

Pooja smiled. "Then you move them to the middle MOFU. This is where they start considering solutions.

They're comparing their options, including your competitors. Your job is to make sure they see the value in what you offer."

Ravi's eyes followed her pen as she continued outlining the funnel. Her voice was so steady, so sure, and the way she explained it made everything click into place.

"And at the bottom," Pooja said, drawing a final circle, "that's the Bottom of Funnel BOFU. This is where they're ready to make a decision. You've done the hard work by nurturing them through the earlier stages. Now, you can pitch your product confidently because they already trust you."

Ravi sat back, staring at the napkin. "I think I've been rushing people to the bottom without doing the work at the top," he admitted. "That's why nothing's sticking."

Pooja nodded. "Exactly. You need to earn their trust before you ask for the sale. It's a process."

For the first time in weeks, Ravi felt a sense of control returning. He finally understood where he had been going wrong, and Pooja had given him the tools to fix it.

"Thanks," he said, looking at her with newfound appreciation. "This is starting to make sense."

Pooja smiled, but there was that flicker again, that unspoken connection that had been building between them all evening. As they finished their meal, the conversation drifted back to lighter topics, but the tension remained, an undercurrent that neither of them addressed directly.

When they left the restaurant, the night air was cool against their skin, the streets quieter now. As they walked side by side, Ravi couldn't help but steal glances at her, wondering if she felt the same pull he did.

At her apartment door, Pooja paused, turning to face him. "We'll pick up where we left off tomorrow?"

"Yeah," Ravi replied, though his mind was miles away from marketing strategy. "Tomorrow."

She smiled, and for a brief moment, Ravi thought she might say something else something that acknowledged the tension hanging between them. But instead, she just nodded and slipped inside, leaving Ravi standing there, his thoughts a jumble of funnels, feelings, and something far more complicated.

As he walked back to his apartment, Ravi couldn't shake the warmth that lingered from their conversation. Business was important, but this whatever was happening between them was starting to feel like something he couldn't ignore any longer.

5. The Paid Ads Dilemma

The following week saw Ravi more focused than ever. His meetings with Pooja had transformed his understanding of his business. He finally felt a sense of direction, thanks to the insights she had provided over the past few weeks. Her ability to break things down so clearly, whether over a simple dinner or during a brainstorming session in his office, had become invaluable to him.

But there was one thing still gnawing at him: his paid ads. No matter how much he tweaked his Google and LinkedIn Ads campaigns, they weren't yielding the results he wanted. Frustrated, he shot a text to Pooja.

Ravi: *Need some help with these paid ads. Can we go over them together?*

Pooja replied quickly, as she often did: *Sure, how about I stop by your office tomorrow?*

The next day, she arrived carrying a laptop bag slung over her shoulder and, to Ravi's surprise, a bag of takeout. "I figured you're probably running on empty," she smiled, placing the containers on his desk. The familiar scent of noodles and spices wafted through the room. The gesture was simple, but it made his office feel less like a sterile workplace and more like a comfortable place to unwind.

"Thanks," Ravi muttered, grateful for the distraction but his mind still stuck on the ad numbers. "I've been trying to make this work, but it feels like I'm just pouring money down the drain."

Pooja moved her chair beside his and leaned in to examine the data on his laptop. As she did, her shoulder brushed lightly against his, and Ravi froze for just a second, his senses momentarily focused on the faint scent of her perfume. It was subtle but distinct, floral with a hint of something fresh, and it hung in the air between them, making him all too aware of how close they were.

He pushed the thought aside, shifting his focus to the task at hand. "I just don't get it," he said, waving a hand at the screen. "I've tried everything. Why isn't this working?"

Pooja, ever the problem-solver, took control of the laptop and began navigating through the data. "Let's take a look at who's clicking on these ads. If the targeting's off, we're wasting money."

Ravi watched as she expertly maneuvered through his Google Ads dashboard, drilling down into the details he'd been overlooking. "You're targeting too broadly," she said after a moment. "Your audience is all over the place. You need to narrow it down focus on the people who fit your ideal customer profile."

He nodded, though truthfully, his attention was wavering. It wasn't that the information wasn't important he knew it was but as Pooja worked beside him, her focus intense and her movements deliberate, he found himself studying her instead. The way her brow furrowed as she concentrated, the quick movements of her fingers on the keyboard, the way she absentmindedly placed a pen between her teeth when she was deep in thought.

Then, with a quick gesture, she tied her hair back with a rubber band. It was something he'd seen her do a hundred times, but in this moment, it felt almost intimate.

Ravi's mind flashed back to their last meeting at the restaurant. There had been a moment a fleeting moment when their hands had brushed, and he'd felt a spark of something between them. Pooja had quickly diverted the conversation back to business, but the feeling had lingered. Now, sitting so close to her, Ravi felt that same tension, like something was simmering just beneath the surface.

"See, here's where you're losing them," Pooja's voice pulled him back to the present. "Your messaging it's not speaking directly to your audience's pain points. You're trying to cast too wide a net, and that's why it's not resonating."

She continued talking, laying out her recommendations for refining his targeting and ad copy, but Ravi was finding it harder to concentrate. His gaze drifted to her again her focus, her calm demeanor, and the way her voice softened as she explained the nuances of ad strategy. For a second, he wondered if she could feel the same pull he was starting to feel.

There was a brief silence as they both stared at the screen. Without thinking, Ravi shifted slightly, his knee brushing against hers. It was a small, accidental touch, but the spark he felt was undeniable.

Pooja's eyes flickered toward him, but she quickly turned back to the screen, her posture a little stiffer now. She cleared her throat and continued, "The key is refining your audience. We've talked about your ICP you need to make sure your ads are speaking directly to them."

Ravi nodded, but his thoughts were scattered. Was she feeling this, too? Or was he imagining it?

Pooja, for her part, was trying to stay professional. But there was no denying that she'd noticed the shift in Ravi's behavior over the last few weeks. He'd started looking at her differently, lingering on her words, his eyes occasionally drifting in a way that made her stomach flutter. She wasn't blind to it she just didn't know how to respond.

She felt it again now, sitting so close to him in the dimly lit office. His knee had barely grazed hers, but the heat from that small touch still lingered. Pooja quickly turned her attention back to the laptop, trying to push the thought from her mind. This was business. This was her job. And Ravi was just another client. At least, that's what she kept telling herself.

"Here," she said, her voice a little tighter now as she pulled up his LinkedIn Ads dashboard. "Let's tweak this copy too. You've got to focus on value, not just features."

Ravi leaned in again, closer this time, trying to pay attention to what she was saying, but his mind was swirling. There was something unspoken between them, something neither of them had fully acknowledged but that hung heavy in the air.

Pooja quickly finished her adjustments, her fingers moving rapidly over the keyboard. "There," she said, her tone more businesslike now. "That should help refine your targeting."

She glanced up at Ravi and saw the look in his eyes intense, curious, as if he was about to say something. For a moment, her breath caught, and she wondered if he would. But she wasn't ready for that. Not yet.

"Anyway," she said, standing abruptly and brushing invisible dust off her jeans. "I should get going. You've got enough to work with here. Keep an eye on the metrics and let me know if you need anything else."

Ravi blinked, the moment slipping away as quickly as it had appeared. He stood too, unsure of what to say. "Thanks, Pooja. I appreciate it."

But the warmth between them was already fading, replaced by an awkward tension that neither of them knew how to navigate.

Pooja smiled, but it didn't reach her eyes. "No problem. Let me know how the ads perform."

And with that, she was gone, leaving Ravi standing in his office, the weight of their unspoken connection heavy in the air.

Pooja's mind was racing as she walked back to her car. The tension she'd felt in that office was undeniable, but so was her discomfort. She liked Ravi he was smart, ambitious, and, admittedly, easy to be around. But this… this was different. This was crossing a line she wasn't sure she wanted to cross.

It was business. That's what she kept reminding herself. He was a client. And she wasn't about to risk her professional reputation over a few lingering glances and accidental touches. But even as she thought it, Pooja couldn't shake the feeling that maybe, just maybe, she was doing something wrong.

When she got home, she stared at her phone, a text from Ravi sitting unopened on her screen. She didn't know what to say, so she didn't respond. Not right away, at least.

Ravi, meanwhile, was left in a fog of confusion. Over the next few days, he replayed their meeting over and over in his head. Had he crossed a line? Was it something he had done or said that had made her pull away? He sent her a few messages, updates on the ads, but her responses were slow, brief, almost perfunctory. Something had shifted, and Ravi couldn't figure out what it was.

For the next few days, they both kept their distance, retreating into their own thoughts, unsure of how to move forward. Ravi busied himself with his business, his investors, his endless meetings, but his thoughts kept drifting back to Pooja.

Pooja, on the other hand, found herself second-guessing every move she made, every word she typed in response to his messages. Was she being too distant? Too cold? Or was this exactly what she needed to do to keep things professional?

Neither of them knew the answer. And for now, neither of them was willing to ask the question.

6. Content Marketing and Confessions

The days that followed their awkward office encounter were slow and filled with a silence that both Ravi and Pooja hadn't anticipated. Their usual ease in conversation had disappeared, replaced by distant responses and brief, professional texts. Ravi felt the weight of their last meeting hang between them, while Pooja, on her end, tried to focus on work, attempting to keep things strictly business.

But the distance wasn't doing either of them any good.

Late one evening, after a long day of meetings and revisions, Ravi found himself pacing his apartment. He couldn't stop thinking about Pooja, her sudden change in behaviour, and the growing tension he couldn't shake. He finally forced himself to text her:

Ravi: *Hey, I think we should talk. I miss our flow, and we still have that content marketing strategy to work on.*

There was a pause, and then Pooja's reply came through: *You're right. Want to come over? I could use a break too. We'll talk.*

Later that night, Ravi found himself standing outside Pooja's apartment building, feeling a mix of nerves and anticipation. He had been to her place before, and something about being on her turf made him feel out of his element. When she buzzed him in, he made his way up, wondering how this conversation would go.

Pooja greeted him with a soft smile when he reached her door. She seemed more relaxed, like the tension between them had eased. "Come on in," she said, stepping aside. "I figured we'd head up to the rooftop. It's quiet and the night's too nice to waste indoors."

They grabbed a bottle of wine and two glasses before making their way upstairs. The rooftop was lit by soft lights, with a cozy seating area tucked into the corner, surrounded by plants and a clear view of the city skyline. The night air was cool, and Ravi immediately felt a sense of calm settle over him as they sat down.

"I know things have been a bit weird lately," Pooja started, pouring them each a glass of wine. "I guess we both got caught up in work and… other things."

Ravi nodded, taking a sip of his wine as he stared out at the lights twinkling across the city. "Yeah. I think I overthought things too. I don't want to make this complicated, Pooja. You've been a big part of helping me grow my business, and I don't want to ruin that."

She smiled, a little more warmly this time. "I know. But let's not stress tonight. Let's talk about what we're good at content marketing."

They spent the next hour discussing Ravi's business and how content marketing could help him grow his brand beyond the paid ads and short-term tactics he'd been focusing on. Pooja, with her usual clarity, explained that content marketing wasn't just about pushing products; it was about building relationships.

"You need to think long-term," she said, leaning back in her chair, her eyes soft but serious. "Blog posts, case studies, white-papers they aren't going to bring instant leads, but they'll establish trust. People buy from people they trust, especially in the B2B space."

Ravi nodded, realising he'd been too focused on the quick wins—ads, promotions, and sales campaigns. "But how do I keep up with it?" he asked. "It sounds like a lot of work, and I'm already swamped."

Pooja took a sip of her wine, her eyes thoughtful. "It *is* a lot of work, but it's worth it. The key is consistency. You have to stay visible, keep sharing valuable content, and build your credibility over time. It's like planting seeds eventually, they'll grow into something bigger."

She explained how Ravi could create a content calendar, breaking down topics into manageable pieces. Blog posts that shared industry insights, case studies that showcased his success stories, and white-papers that offered in-depth solutions to his clients' pain points. "It's about showing them that you understand their challenges and that you've got the solutions they need."

Ravi listened, absorbing every word. Pooja had a way of making even the most complex strategies sound simple. And, more than that, she made him believe in the process.

"I get it," Ravi said, nodding slowly. "It's a slow burn, but it's what builds a solid foundation."

As the conversation moved between content strategies and personal stories from the early days of their careers, the mood began to shift. The night air grew cooler, and Ravi noticed how comfortable it felt being there, sharing stories and ideas with Pooja. The more they talked, the more he realised how much he'd missed these moments with her.

Eventually, the conversation drifted toward their college days—back when they were both still figuring out who they were and what they wanted. The memories made Ravi nostalgic, and perhaps it was the wine, or maybe the comfort of the rooftop, but something emboldened him.

"Do you remember our last year of college?" he asked, a small smile playing on his lips.

Pooja laughed, looking up at the stars. "How could I forget? We were both so stressed about our futures. I was freaking out about my marketing degree, and you were… what was it? Trying to juggle five side hustles at once?"

Ravi chuckled. "Yeah, something like that." He paused, swirling his wine in his glass before continuing, his voice softer. "I never told you this back then, but… I had feelings for you."

The words hung in the air between them, and for a moment, neither of them spoke. Pooja turned to look at him, her eyes wide with surprise. "What?" she asked, her voice barely above a whisper.

Ravi felt his heart pounding, but he pressed on. "Yeah… I didn't know how to say it back then. We were such good friends, and I didn't want to mess that up. So I just… kept quiet."

Pooja's lips curved into a small smile, and she shook her head, almost in disbelief. "I had no idea. But… if we're being honest, I kind of felt the same way. I just didn't think you were interested."

Ravi laughed softly, feeling a mix of relief and regret. "Guess we were both clueless, huh?"

The atmosphere between them changed there was something warm, unspoken, but undeniably present. Pooja looked away for a moment, as if gathering her thoughts. "But we've come so far since then," she said, her voice gentle. "We've got a business to scale, Ravi. There's a lot at stake now."

He nodded, understanding what she was saying but still feeling the weight of their shared confession. "Yeah, I get that. But… I just thought you should know. It's been on my mind."

Pooja glanced at him, her smile soft but knowing. "Well, thanks for telling me. Maybe things would've been different back then, but we've got different priorities now." She paused, then added with a playful grin, "Like getting your content strategy in order."

Ravi laughed, feeling the tension ease. But even as they returned to business talk, the confession lingered in the air, a reminder of the connection they'd always had but never fully acknowledged.

As the evening wore on, Pooja helped Ravi map out a plan to start producing regular content. They discussed topics that would resonate with his audience insights into his industry, practical tips for business owners, and case studies that highlighted his success stories.

"Content marketing isn't about selling right away," Pooja reminded him. "It's about educating your audience, showing them that you understand their problems and that you're the expert they can trust."

Ravi nodded, feeling more confident now that he had a plan. With Pooja's guidance, he started to see how powerful content could be not just for generating leads but for building long-term relationships with his audience.

"And the best part?" Pooja added with a wink. "Once your content starts gaining traction, it'll keep working for you, even when you're not actively promoting it. That's the magic of content marketing it's like having an evergreen sales tool."

By the time they finished their wine and said goodnight, Ravi felt a sense of clarity, both about his business and his relationship with Pooja. The confession had been unexpected, but in a way, it had cleared the air between them, allowing them to move forward professionally, and maybe, someday, personally.

As Ravi headed home that night, he couldn't stop smiling. He finally had a content strategy in place and felt more connected to Pooja than ever before. They had a business to scale, sure, but perhaps there was still room for more between them only time would tell.

7. Cold Outreach and Hot Feelings

The rooftop confession between Ravi and Pooja had added a subtle but undeniable layer of complexity to their relationship. They hadn't revisited that moment, choosing instead to keep their interactions professional. But beneath the surface, emotions simmered. Both Ravi and Pooja danced around their feelings, as if waiting for the other to take the next step.

With the content marketing strategy yielding early signs of success for Ravi's SaaS product, his startup was slowly gaining traction. Blog posts, case studies, and social media updates were driving engagement. Yet, one crucial part of the process still made Ravi uneasy cold outreach. It wasn't that he didn't understand its importance but he hated the thought of sending impersonal messages to people he had never met, trying to sell them something without a connection.

One evening, after another long day, Ravi texted Pooja. He couldn't shake the frustration and felt like he was hitting a wall.

Ravi: "Cold outreach is the worst. Can't wrap my head around it. Got time to save me?"

Her response was quick, almost as if she'd been waiting for an excuse to see him: *Pooja*: "Of course, but only if there's coffee first and wine after. See you at 7? 😉"

As usual, Pooja brought her characteristic enthusiasm and warmth, and Ravi felt the familiar mix of anticipation and nerves. It wasn't just about business anymore.

That evening, Ravi sat at his desk, trying not to overthink things as Pooja arrived, carrying a small bag and a smile that made his heart skip. "You look like you're gearing up for war," she joked, setting her bag down and pulling out her laptop. "Relax, it's just cold outreach, not a battlefield."

Ravi chuckled but felt the tension ease a little. "Feels the same sometimes. I just can't shake the feeling that I'm bothering people when I send these messages."

Pooja took a seat next to him, closer than usual. "You're not bothering anyone," she said, her voice gentle but firm. "You're offering something valuable. The key is to show them that. People respond when they feel understood, when the message feels like it's for them not just another mass email."

As she spoke, Ravi could feel the warmth of her presence beside him. She leaned in slightly, eyes scanning his screen as she read over his first draft. The proximity was charged, their shoulders brushing lightly, and though the conversation was focused on business, the undercurrent of something more made the moment feel... electric.

"Okay, so here's what we do," Pooja said, interrupting his thoughts. "Let's take a look at their profiles. See if you can find anything personal like a recent post they shared or a milestone they reached. Start with that."

Ravi typed as she spoke, following her lead. "You mean, like a conversation starter?"

"Exactly," Pooja replied, her tone playful. "Think of it like... breaking the ice. But be subtle. People can sense when you're trying too hard."

Ravi smirked. "Kind of like how I shouldn't try too hard to impress someone?"

Pooja raised an eyebrow, catching the slight flirtation in his words. "Something like that," she said, her lips curving into a small smile. "Just enough to get their attention, but not so much that you seem desperate."

Their conversation danced on the edge of business and something personal, each word carrying a dual meaning that hung in the air between them. Ravi couldn't help but wonder if they were still talking about cold outreach at all.

Hours passed, and they worked seamlessly together. Each time Ravi doubted himself, Pooja was there to nudge him in the right direction sometimes literally. When he hesitated over a message, she leaned in, giving him a playful nudge with her shoulder, her hand lingering on his arm a fraction too long.

"You've got this," she whispered, her breath warm against his skin. "Just trust yourself."

Ravi nodded, typing with renewed confidence. The sound of their typing filled the room, but the tension between them remained thick, like an unsaid question waiting to be asked.

At one point, Pooja passed him a cup of coffee, their hands brushing for just a moment longer than necessary. It was a small gesture, but the touch sent a spark through Ravi, one he knew Pooja felt too. Her smile confirmed it a knowing look that said they were both very aware of the growing connection between them.

"See?" Pooja said as they finished the last batch of messages. "It's all about personalisation. When people feel seen, they're more likely to respond. You're not just pitching a product you're starting a conversation."

Ravi nodded, impressed with how easily she made everything seem. "You really have a knack for this," he admitted, leaning back in his chair. "I think I've been going about it all wrong."

Pooja laughed softly. "Well, you've got me now. We'll get those leads rolling in soon enough."

Her words were meant to reassure him, but there was a teasing lilt in her voice, one that made Ravi's heart race just a little faster. They locked eyes for a moment, and something unspoken passed between them. It wasn't just about the work anymore.

"Thanks for all this," Ravi said, his voice quieter than before. "I don't think I could've done it without you."

Pooja looked at him, her smile softening. "That's what I'm here for, right? To help you succeed... in business."

Her pause was brief but loaded with implication. It was as if she wanted to say something more but stopped herself. Ravi caught the subtle change in her tone, and for a brief moment, he wondered if now was the time to finally address what had been building between them.

Before he could say anything, Pooja shifted the conversation back to business, her voice light and teasing again. "But don't get too comfortable. Once those leads start coming in, you'll have even more work to do."

Ravi grinned, playing along. "More work, huh? You sure you're not just trying to keep me around longer?"

Pooja laughed, her eyes twinkling with mischief. "Maybe. Or maybe I just enjoy watching you sweat a little."

They wrapped up the session, and as they stood to stretch, Pooja leaned against the desk, watching him with a thoughtful expression. "You've come a long way, you know," she said softly. "When we first started, you were so unsure of everything. But now... you're handling things like a pro."

Ravi met her gaze, feeling a swell of gratitude. "I had a good teacher."

Pooja's smile was warm, but there was something else there, too something deeper. "You've always had it in you, Ravi. You just needed someone to remind you of that."

For a moment, the air between them felt charged again, like it had on the rooftop that night. The weight of unsaid words pressed down on them both, but just as Ravi felt the pull to say something more, Pooja stepped back, breaking the spell.

"We should celebrate," she said, her tone suddenly lighter. "Wine?"

Ravi chuckled, relieved by the shift in mood. "I thought you'd never ask."

As they sipped their wine, sitting close on the couch, the atmosphere shifted from work to something more relaxed. Pooja leaned back, her eyes scanning the room before landing on Ravi. "You know," she said, her voice soft but playful, "cold outreach is a lot like flirting. You've got to be bold enough to make the first move but patient enough to wait for the right response."

Ravi raised an eyebrow, intrigued by her analogy. "So... are you saying I should flirt more with my leads?"

Pooja laughed, shaking her head. "No, not exactly. But think of it this way when you're reaching out, you're trying to make a connection. You've got to find common ground, keep it light, and leave them wanting more."

Ravi smirked, leaning in slightly. "And what happens when they respond?"

Pooja's eyes twinkled with amusement. "That's when the real fun begins."

Their conversation was layered, half about business, half about something else entirely. Ravi wasn't sure where the lines blurred anymore, but he wasn't in a hurry to figure it out. There was something thrilling about the ambiguity, the push and pull between them.

As the night wore on, they continued talking about leads, about business, and occasionally, about things that had nothing to do with either. The dual meanings in their words danced between them, each playful remark charged with deeper significance.

By the time Pooja stood to leave, the tension had reached a comfortable simmer, and Ravi found himself reluctant to say goodnight.

"Same time tomorrow?" Pooja asked with a teasing smile as she grabbed her bag.

Ravi nodded, feeling lighter than he had in days. "Wouldn't miss it."

As she walked to the door, she turned back with one last playful look. "Don't get too comfortable, Ravi. Business first, remember?"

But the smile she gave him before leaving hinted that maybe just maybe business wouldn't always be the only thing on their minds.

8. Partnership and a Turning Point

The morning sun filtered through the blinds of Ravi's small apartment, casting long, golden rays across his desk. His thoughts were still lingering on the previous evening with Pooja. There was an undeniable shift between them, something deeper than before. But there was no time to dwell Pooja was coming over again today, and they had work to do.

Ravi sipped his coffee, his mind racing as he tried to shake off the distraction of the night before. Business first. But every time he thought about Pooja's teasing smile, he found it harder to keep things strictly professional. He glanced at his calendar, the glaring reminder of today's meeting.

Just as he began to organize his notes, there was a knock at the door. His heart raced for a moment before he composed himself and opened it to find Pooja standing there, all smiles and energy, holding her laptop.

"Ready for round two?" she asked, breezing in like a breath of fresh air. There was an easy confidence in the way she moved, like the unspoken tension between them last night hadn't phased her at all. Ravi admired her ability to keep things light, even when their connection felt anything but.

He smiled, pushing thoughts of last night aside. "Let's do this."

They settled in, the atmosphere comfortable but charged with a subtle undercurrent of something more. As they dove into brainstorming, Pooja, always full of ideas, proposed something that immediately grabbed Ravi's attention.

"Why don't we partner with a complementary company to co-host an event? It'll help us tap into a whole new audience," she suggested, her fingers flying over her laptop keys as she spoke.

Ravi leaned forward, intrigued. "What kind of event are you thinking?"

"A webinar," she said confidently. "We focus on mid-sized business owners, offer them practical insights on scaling with SaaS tools like yours, and invite a guest speaker from another company maybe someone who deals with financial solutions or business automation. It'll show how your product fits into a larger ecosystem."

Ravi's eyes lit up. "That's brilliant. We can cross-promote it with the partner company and tap into their audience. Double the exposure."

Pooja grinned. "Exactly. It's all about amplifying the reach. We'll need to plan everything, though topics, speakers, marketing. But I know we can pull it off."

They spent the next few hours outlining their approach. Pooja's enthusiasm was infectious, and Ravi found himself energized by her ideas. As they worked side by side, their bond grew deeper, fueled by the seamless way they complemented each other. Pooja's creativity balanced Ravi's strategic thinking, and together, they were building something promising not just for the business, but for themselves.

Days passed quickly, with both of them focused on organizing the webinar. They secured a partner company that specialized in business automation software and planned the event to appeal to mid-sized businesses, promising actionable tips on growth strategies. As the details came together, the excitement was palpable. Registrations were already rolling in, and the webinar looked like it would be a hit.

As the date of the webinar drew closer, Ravi found himself spending more and more time with Pooja. Late-night calls to finalize marketing plans, shared spreadsheets with target lists, and even impromptu brainstorming sessions over coffee had become the norm. But each time they met, the tension between them became harder to ignore.

The night before the webinar, they met at Pooja's apartment to finalize the last-minute details. It was cozy inside, the soft lighting making everything feel a little more intimate than usual. Ravi could feel the weight of the moment as soon as he walked in.

Pooja handed him a cup of tea, and they sat close on her couch, laptops open as they reviewed the presentation slides. The work was steady, but there was a certain ease between them that neither could deny. Every time their hands brushed while passing the laptop, or their eyes met across the room, the air seemed to crackle with unspoken words.

As they reached the final slide, Ravi closed his laptop and leaned back, exhaling deeply. "That's it," he said, his voice a little quieter now that the work was done. "We're ready."

Pooja nodded, but she wasn't looking at the screen. Her gaze lingered on Ravi, a soft smile playing on her lips. "You've come a long way since we started this, you know."

He met her eyes, and for the first time in a long while, he let himself acknowledge what had been building between them. "I couldn't have done it without you," he admitted, his voice low and sincere.

The room fell silent, the tension thick between them. Pooja's smile softened, and her hand, which had been resting on the couch, moved just a little closer to his. There was no hiding it anymore they were both feeling the same thing.

Ravi hesitated for a moment, unsure if this was the right time. But then again, when would it ever feel right? The air was heavy with the weight of everything unspoken between them, and he wasn't sure he could let it pass again.

He leaned in, slowly, testing the waters. Pooja didn't pull away. In fact, she leaned in too, her breath soft against his skin. And then, before he could second-guess himself, he kissed her.

It was soft at first, tentative, as if they were both testing the boundaries of this new dynamic. But as her lips moved against his, the kiss deepened, becoming something neither of them could stop. It felt like a release of all the tension that had been building between them for weeks.

When they finally pulled apart, both of them were breathless, the room suddenly feeling a little smaller.

For a moment, they didn't speak. They just looked at each other, trying to process what had just happened.

Pooja was the first to break the silence, her voice soft but steady. "Ravi... we need to talk."

He nodded, knowing she was right. As much as he wanted to hold on to the moment, there were things they needed to figure out.

"I don't want to complicate things," she continued, her eyes searching his. "We've got something good going here—both with the business and... this. But mixing the two can be tricky."

Ravi ran a hand through his hair, his mind racing. "I know," he said quietly. "But I can't pretend this isn't happening."

Pooja smiled, but there was a hint of uncertainty in her eyes. "I don't want to pretend either. But maybe we should take it slow? Focus on the webinar first, see where things go from there?"

Ravi nodded, relieved that she wasn't pushing him away. "I can do slow."

They shared a soft laugh, the tension between them easing just a little. For now, they had an understanding. The business came first, but whatever was growing between them it wasn't going away.

The next day, the webinar went off without a hitch. Ravi and Pooja co-hosted with the partner company, and the turnout exceeded their expectations. The content was engaging, the questions from the audience thoughtful, and by the end of the session, Ravi could feel the momentum building.

The partnership strategy had worked wonders. Not only had they amplified their reach by tapping into the partner company's audience, but the collaboration had brought a level of credibility to Ravi's product that he hadn't anticipated. The leads came pouring in, and it was clear that this was just the beginning.

As they wrapped up the event, Ravi glanced over at Pooja. She was smiling, proud of the work they'd done together. But there was something else in her eyes too a softness, a recognition of the moment they shared last night.

The turning point wasn't just about the business anymore. It was about them, too.

9. Scaling Up - Ravi's Transformation

The office buzzed with energy as Ravi stepped inside, a sense of pride swelling in his chest. The webinar had been a massive success, drawing in leads that had him smiling as he reviewed his growing sales funnel. Each new inquiry felt like a step forward not just for his business but for his journey as an entrepreneur.

Pooja had been by his side through it all, her presence a constant source of motivation and inspiration. They had navigated the treacherous waters of starting a new venture together, and now that their relationship had evolved into something more, it added a new layer of complexity to their dynamic. They were both aware of the line they had to walk, balancing their personal and professional lives. Yet, there was an undeniable thrill in it all each meeting, each brainstorming session became charged with an electric connection that neither could deny.

As he settled down at his desk, Ravi's thoughts drifted to Pooja. She was always the voice of reason, pushing him to focus on the bigger picture. He recalled their late-night conversations, where they'd laugh and plan, dissecting ideas and strategies with equal parts seriousness and playfulness. Her marketing expertise had helped him refine his approach and think creatively about their brand.

"Ravi!" Pooja called as she walked into the office, her energy infectious. "You won't believe the feedback we've received from the webinar! Everyone is raving about the insights we shared. It's a game changer!"

He turned to her, the smile on his face matching her enthusiasm. "I couldn't have done it without you. Your ideas brought everything to life. You're amazing, you know that?"

Pooja's cheeks flushed slightly, and she brushed a strand of hair behind her ear, a playful smile tugging at her lips. "Well, I do have a knack for turning boring content into something exciting. But let's not forget the incredible SaaS product you've built. It's a game changer in itself."

Their banter flowed effortlessly, a comfortable rhythm built on mutual respect and burgeoning affection. As they stood close, reviewing the metrics from the webinar, Ravi felt a warmth spread through him. He'd gone from a stressed entrepreneur on the brink of failure to a confident business owner with a clear vision and he attributed so much of that growth to Pooja.

Later that day, as they worked on finalizing their next marketing campaign, Ravi found himself reflecting on the transformation he had undergone. He remembered sleepless nights spent worrying about his startup, the constant fear of failure hanging over him like a dark cloud. But now, things felt different. He had clarity. He had Pooja, and together, they were building something that had the potential to last.

"Hey, can I ask you something?" Ravi turned to Pooja, curiosity brimming in his eyes.

"Of course," she replied, tilting her head slightly, her gaze steady.

"What do you think has been the most important lesson for us in this journey so far?"

Pooja considered for a moment, her brow furrowing slightly. "I think it's about the process. We've learned to stay customer-centric. Every time we've focused on what our customers need, instead of what we think they need, we've seen results."

Ravi nodded, absorbing her words. "You're right. Building a business is like building a relationship. It's all about trust, consistency, and long-term commitment."

"Exactly," she said, her eyes sparkling with passion. "When we prioritize our customers, we not only meet their needs but also build loyalty. They become advocates for our brand."

He admired her intellect and the way she could dissect complex ideas into simple truths. It was one of the many reasons he had fallen for her. In that moment, he leaned closer, his heart racing. "And what about us?" he asked, his voice softening. "What's our process?"

Pooja's eyes widened slightly, surprise flickering across her face before a teasing smile broke through. "Well, I'd say we need to focus on trust and communication," she replied, a playful glint in her eye. "And maybe some romantic dinners sprinkled in?"

"Romantic dinners? I can definitely get on board with that," he chuckled, his heart fluttering at her flirty tone.

Their eyes locked, the moment stretching out as an unspoken understanding passed between them. Ravi felt the gravity of their connection deepening he cherished the blend of professional respect and personal affection they had cultivated.

As the days went by, the excitement of their business growth blended seamlessly with their evolving relationship. They began to carve out time for each other outside of work, indulging in cozy dinners and late-night strolls. Each shared moment brought them closer, and Ravi found himself entranced by Pooja's laughter and the way her eyes sparkled when she talked about her dreams.

One evening, they decided to take a break from their usual routine. Pooja suggested they go to a nearby art exhibition, something neither of them had done in a while. As they walked through the gallery, admiring the vibrant paintings, Ravi felt a sense of freedom. The chaos of the past seemed miles away.

"Look at this one," Pooja said, gesturing toward a colorful abstract piece. "It's chaotic yet beautiful, don't you think?"

Ravi stepped closer, admiring the swirls of color that danced across the canvas. "It's like a representation of our journey," he remarked, glancing sideways at her. "Chaotic but beautiful."

Pooja laughed softly, her eyes twinkling. "That's a perfect way to describe it. And I have to say, I like this kind of chaos."

They moved through the gallery, sharing playful commentary on the art, each moment deepening their connection. Ravi felt lighter than he had in a long time, the weight of responsibility lifting as he lost himself in Pooja's presence.

As they stood in front of a particularly striking piece, Ravi turned to her, the moment feeling charged with possibility. "Pooja, can I ask you something?"

"Anything," she replied, her tone inviting.

"If we're building this business together, do you think we could build a life together too?"

Pooja's breath caught slightly, her eyes wide with surprise. But then, a soft smile broke through her initial shock. "Ravi, I'd like that. But let's keep focusing on our business for now. We can't forget about the process," she teased, her playful tone lightening the moment.

Ravi chuckled, feeling a warmth spread through him. "Fair enough. But just know that I'm in it for the long haul both in business and in life."

As they left the gallery, hand in hand, Ravi knew this was just the beginning. He was scaling up not just in business but in his relationship with Pooja. Each step forward felt exhilarating, filled with the promise of what was to come. Together, they were building something extraordinary, one day at a time.

The following week brought even more validation for Ravi and Pooja. Ravi's investor, Mr. Kapoor, had scheduled a meeting to discuss their recent success. As Ravi prepared for the conversation, he couldn't shake off the excitement mixed with nervousness. He wanted to impress Mr. Kapoor with the results of their latest marketing efforts.

When the day finally arrived, Mr. Kapoor entered the conference room, a wide smile on his face. "Ravi, I must say, I'm impressed! Your company's transformation in such a short time is remarkable. How did you do it?"

Ravi exchanged a glance with Pooja, who was sitting beside him, exuding confidence. "Thank you, Mr. Kapoor. I'd like you to meet Pooja, my college friend and marketing consultant. She's been instrumental in refining our strategies and has her own business that complements our vision perfectly."

Mr. Kapoor turned to Pooja, extending his hand. "It's a pleasure to meet you, Pooja. I've heard a lot about the innovative strategies Ravi has implemented. Your expertise must have played a significant role in that."

Pooja smiled, shaking his hand firmly. "Thank you, Mr. Kapoor. It's great to meet you. Ravi and I have been collaborating closely to ensure our marketing approach resonates with our audience."

"I can see that," Mr. Kapoor said, nodding approvingly. "Ravi, having someone with Pooja's experience on your side is a tremendous asset. It's fantastic to see how you both are not just building a product but a community around it. That's what true entrepreneurship is about. I'd love to hear more about your future plans."

As Ravi and Pooja shared their vision for the upcoming months, Ravi felt a rush of pride. They were not just surviving; they were thriving. Mr. Kapoor's appreciation of their work added to the buoyancy he felt every day.

Once the meeting concluded, Mr. Kapoor stood up to shake Ravi's hand. "Keep up the great work, Ravi. You're onto something special here." Then he turned to Pooja. "And you, Pooja, are a crucial part of this success. Don't underestimate your impact."

Ravi watched as Pooja beamed under Mr. Kapoor's praise. In that moment, he realized how lucky he was to have her by his side not just as a friend but as a vital support in this journey.

That night, after a long day of meetings, Ravi and Pooja found themselves lounging in a cozy café. The atmosphere buzzed with conversations, and the aroma of freshly brewed coffee filled the air. Ravi couldn't shake off the excitement from the day.

"Today was a huge milestone, wasn't it?" he said, his eyes bright with enthusiasm.

Pooja nodded, her gaze thoughtful. "Absolutely. It's a reminder that we're on the right path."

Ravi nodded, his gaze focused on her. "Absolutely. His belief in our vision is a huge boost. But honestly, it's you who keeps me grounded. Your insights are invaluable."

She smiled, her eyes sparkling. "And your determination is contagious. I can't imagine doing this with anyone else."

Their conversation flowed easily, a blend of laughter and deeper reflections on their journey. As the café buzzed around them, Ravi felt an overwhelming sense of gratitude not just for the business success but for the bond they had formed.

As they wrapped up their evening, Ravi leaned in closer. "You know, we make a great team. What do you say we celebrate our wins a little more often?"

Pooja laughed softly, a hint of mischief in her eyes. "I'm all for it! But remember, we can't lose sight of our goals. The process comes first, right?"

Ravi chuckled, nodding. "Yes, the process. But maybe a little celebration won't hurt either. After all, we've earned it!"

With that playful exchange, Ravi felt a renewed sense of purpose. Together, they were not just partners in business but a team ready to take on the world. Each day brought new challenges and victories, but as long as they had each other, Ravi knew they could face anything that came their way.

In the weeks that followed, Ravi and Pooja poured their hearts into the business. They continued to refine their strategies, adapting to market shifts and customer feedback. The partnership evolved seamlessly, as did their relationship, blending professionalism with a deepening personal connection.

With each challenge they overcame, their bond strengthened. It was a remarkable journey, and Ravi felt grateful every day for Pooja's unwavering support. She was not just a colleague or a friend she was the heartbeat of their venture, inspiring him to reach heights he had only dreamed of.

As they prepared for their next big launch, Ravi couldn't help but reflect on how far they had come. The path was far from easy, but with Pooja by his side, he felt invincible. Together, they were ready to soar, hand in hand.

10. A New Beginning

The celebratory dinner was supposed to be just that a way to mark their success. But as Ravi and Pooja stepped into the elegant restaurant, there was a different energy between them. The air seemed warmer, filled with anticipation, as if this night was about more than just the business win they had worked so hard for.

They were shown to a quiet corner table, the dim lighting casting soft shadows, creating a cozy, intimate atmosphere. As Pooja sat down across from him, Ravi couldn't help but admire her. She had always been striking, but tonight, there was something different an effortless grace, a quiet confidence that radiated from her. And it wasn't just about her business acumen; it was about her, the woman who had supported him through his darkest hours and pushed him toward his greatest victories.

He grinned as he leaned back in his chair, letting the moment settle. "You know, I've been thinking," he started, a playful glint in his eyes, "I might have to keep finding excuses to get us into these fancy dinners. Who knew business success came with perks like this?"

Pooja raised an eyebrow, leaning in slightly. "Oh, is that so? You think I'm only here for the fancy food?"

Ravi chuckled, shaking his head. "Well, I wasn't going to say it out loud, but now that you mention it…"

She laughed, her eyes sparkling. "If you think you can impress me with a few candlelit dinners, you've got a lot to learn, Mr. CEO."

Ravi leaned in, his tone dropping a notch, voice playful yet sincere. "Impressing you has always been the goal, but I guess I'll have to step up my game then."

Pooja smirked, playing along. "You might want to focus on something other than work, for starters."

"Is that your professional advice as a consultant?" Ravi asked, with a teasing smile.

She grinned, leaning back, crossing her arms playfully. "Let's just say… I'm not used to mixing business with pleasure. It's a fine line, you know."

"Maybe," Ravi said, his tone softening, the teasing giving way to something deeper. "But I think we're both a little past that line, don't you?"

For a moment, the air between them thickened, and the light-hearted banter shifted into something more profound. Pooja didn't respond immediately, and Ravi wondered if he'd pushed too far. But then she smiled, a softer, more vulnerable smile that made his heart race.

"Maybe we are," she admitted, her voice barely above a whisper.

Ravi reached out, taking her hand gently across the table. He looked at her, his thumb brushing the back of her hand, and for the first time that night, they weren't just colleagues, they weren't just friends they were two people standing on the edge of something more.

"You know," Ravi started, his voice quieter now, "all this time I've been chasing success, trying to build this company, I didn't realize the best thing that's happened to me wasn't just about the business."

Pooja's breath caught slightly, her eyes locked on his. "What do you mean?"

"I mean… you. You came into my life when everything was falling apart. You didn't just help me fix my business you helped me find something worth fighting for. I think I've been too scared to admit it."

Pooja's eyes softened, her hand tightening around his. She looked at him for a long moment, her expression unreadable at first, but then she smiled a soft, knowing smile that told him she felt it too.

"I didn't expect this either," she confessed. "Coming here, I thought I was just helping an old friend. But… somewhere along the way, it became more than that. It's more than business now, Ravi."

Ravi felt his heart swell at her words. He hadn't been prepared for this depth of feeling that had slowly crept up on him. They had always been friends, yes, but somewhere between late-night strategy sessions and shared victories, something had shifted. Something had blossomed.

"You know," Ravi said, his tone lighter but still filled with emotion, "we're going to have to figure out how to balance this. Business and… us."

Pooja laughed softly, shaking her head. "It's not going to be easy, is it?"

"No," Ravi admitted. "But then again, nothing worth having ever is."

Their meals arrived, but the conversation stayed light as they laughed and flirted, both aware of the new energy between them, yet comfortable in it. They spoke of everything from the successes of the company to shared memories from their college days.

But as the night drew to a close, their conversation grew quieter, more intimate. They both knew that this wasn't just about the business anymore. They were both aware that something had changed between them a deepening connection that had been simmering beneath the surface for months, now finally breaking through.

"Do you ever think," Pooja said quietly, "about how different things could've been if I hadn't come back? If I hadn't stepped in when I did?"

Ravi looked at her, his gaze intense. "All the time. If you hadn't come back, I might've lost the business. But more than that… I might've lost something even more important."

Pooja's eyes shimmered, her breath catching as she realized the depth of his words. He wasn't just talking about the company anymore he was talking about her. About them.

"You didn't lose me," she whispered. "I'm here. And I'm not going anywhere."

Ravi felt a lump rise in his throat, his chest tightening with emotion. He had spent so much of his life focusing on work, on success, that he hadn't allowed himself to think about what really mattered. But now, with Pooja here, sitting across from him, he realized that success meant nothing without someone to share it with.

He stood up, gently pulling her up from her seat. "Come on," he said softly.

Pooja looked at him, confused but curious. "Where are we going?"

"You'll see," Ravi said, a small smile playing on his lips.

They walked out of the restaurant, hand in hand, stepping into the cool night air. The city lights glimmered around them, but in that moment, it felt like the world had shrunk to just the two of them.

As they walked down the quiet street, Ravi turned to her, stopping under a streetlamp. The light cast a soft glow over them, and he looked at her, really looked at her, as if seeing her for the first time.

"I don't know what's going to happen next," Ravi admitted, his voice thick with emotion. "With the business, with us. But I do know one thing I don't want to do any of it without you."

Pooja's eyes filled with emotion, her heart racing as she looked at him. "You won't have to," she whispered.

And in that moment, standing under the soft glow of the streetlight, Ravi leaned in, gently brushing his lips against hers. It was a kiss filled with all the emotions they had been holding back for months the fear, the hope, the longing, and the promise of something more.

When they finally pulled away, Pooja smiled, her eyes glistening with unshed tears. "So," she said softly, "what now?"

Ravi smiled, taking her hand again as they started walking down the street, their steps in sync. "Now?" he said, glancing at her. "Now, we face whatever comes next together."

As they walked hand in hand, the future stretched out before them unknown, unpredictable, but full of promise. The challenges of balancing business and love would be there, no doubt. But for the first time in his life, Ravi wasn't afraid. With Pooja by his side, he knew they could face anything.

The success of the company was important, but this what they had was what made it all worthwhile. And as they disappeared into the night, it was clear: their story was just beginning.

Epilogue

As the sun began to set, casting a golden glow across the city skyline, Ravi sat by the window in his office, his sanctuary, a place that had witnessed his lowest points and now, his greatest triumphs. The steady hum of his company filled the background, but tonight was different. Tonight, he was reflecting, not planning.

It was time to speak directly to the people who had been on this journey with him the readers who had seen his transformation from a struggling entrepreneur to a confident business owner, and from a lonely man to someone who had found love.

He looked out at the city, remembering the sleepless nights, the moments of doubt, and the victories that had come with grit and persistence.

"To anyone reading this," Ravi began in his mind, imagining the words flowing from him as if speaking to a close friend, "I want you to know one thing: this wasn't just a story about business. It was a story about growth about learning to embrace change, push past fear, and step outside your comfort zone."

He thought back to the beginning those early days when he had nearly given up. "Success," he continued, "doesn't happen overnight. It's messy, frustrating, and full of setbacks. But it's in those setbacks that you learn the most. Failure isn't the end; it's a teacher. And if you're willing to listen, it will show you the way forward."

Ravi smiled as he remembered Pooja his college friend turned consultant, and now the woman he shared his life with. Her guidance had been instrumental, not just in building his company, but in shaping him into the person he had become.

"One of the most important lessons I've learned," Ravi reflected, "is that you can't do it alone. Whether it's in business or in love, the relationships you nurture are what will sustain you. Surround yourself with people who push you, who challenge you, and who believe in you even when you don't believe in yourself."

He took a deep breath, thinking about all the times Pooja had pushed him outside his comfort zone, reminding him to stay focused on the process and the people he served. She had taught him that business, like love, was built on trust, consistency, and commitment.

"Growth," Ravi mused, "isn't just about scaling up a company or hitting financial goals. It's about becoming the person you're meant to be. It's about evolving, both personally and professionally. And that evolution often requires letting go of old ways of thinking, old fears, and being open to new possibilities."

He looked around his office, remembering how different everything had been just a few years ago. "If there's one thing I want you to take away from my journey, it's this:

success isn't just about what you achieve. It's about who you become along the way."

Ravi knew the journey wasn't over. There would be new challenges, new risks, and new opportunities. But he was ready for them—because he had learned that success isn't a destination. It's a process, a journey, and it requires constant growth, adaptation, and persistence.

"Whether you're building a business, nurturing a relationship, or chasing a dream, remember: it's the willingness to evolve, to keep learning, and to stay committed that makes all the difference. Don't be afraid to fail. Don't be afraid to change. And above all, don't be afraid to love what you do and who you share it with."

He smiled to himself, feeling a deep sense of contentment. The journey had been long and difficult, but it had been worth it. And as he stood up, ready to leave the office and head home to Pooja, he knew that the best was yet to come.

"Here's to the next chapter," Ravi thought, as he turned off the lights and walked out, ready for whatever life had in store.

Acknowledgments

Every journey, no matter how personal or professional, is never truly walked alone. This book, while centered on the story of Ravi and his transformation, is the product of the support, encouragement, and insights of many people.

First, I want to express my deepest gratitude to my readers. Your curiosity, enthusiasm, and belief in this story motivated me through every page. Your support has been the driving force behind this book.

To my family, who have always been my bedrock, thank you for your endless love and unwavering belief in me. Your encouragement in moments of doubt and your patience as I navigated the ups and downs of this project kept me grounded and focused.

A heartfelt thanks to my close friends and colleagues, who provided valuable feedback, ideas, and endless conversations that shaped the direction of this story. You helped me think critically and creatively about the challenges both in business and relationships, and your input was instrumental in crafting this narrative.

To my mentors, past and present, thank you for the lessons you've imparted, both in business and life. You taught me that success isn't just about strategy but also about empathy, resilience, and personal growth. These lessons are woven into every chapter of this book.

A special thanks to **Abhinav Kumhar**, whose incredible talent and vision brought the cover of this book to life.

Your design not only captured the essence of the story but also added a visual layer that connects deeply with readers. Thank you for your hard work and creativity.

Lastly, to everyone who believed in this story, who took the time to offer guidance, support, or simply a kind word—thank you. This book is as much yours as it is mine.

Here's to the heart and hustle that we all invest in the things we believe in.

About Author

Shubham Shaurav is a dynamic entrepreneur, marketing consultant, and author with a proven track record in helping companies scale exponentially. Known for his deep expertise in digital marketing, Shubham has spent over a decade guiding businesses to unprecedented growth through strategic, data-driven, and creative approaches. As the founder of Mind Mozaic, a pioneering marketing agency, he has partnered with a diverse range of B2B and technology companies, using his innovative solutions to turn challenges into opportunities for success.

Shubham's intellectual contributions go beyond his consulting work. He has published several research papers on digital transformation and marketing automation, earning him recognition in the academic and business communities alike. He has also authored two successful non-fiction books, which focus on business growth strategies and modern marketing techniques. Now, with *The Heart of Hustle*—his debut fiction novel—Shubham shifts his focus to the emotional journey behind entrepreneurship.

While this is a work of fiction, Shubham draws on his experiences as an entrepreneur, weaving in the highs and lows of building a business, the pressures from investors, and the complexity of managing personal relationships alongside professional ambitions. *The Heart of Hustle* reflects Shubham's understanding that success is not just about business acumen but about personal growth, trust, and perseverance. Through this book, Shubham brings readers into a world where the lines between professional hustle and personal life blur, offering lessons that resonate far beyond the boardroom.

www.ingramcontent.com/pod-product-compliance
Lightning Source LLC
Chambersburg PA
CBHW031755150726
47989CB00006B/2729